Spiritually Bound

Tiffany Miller

BookLeaf Publishing

Presentation by *BookLeaf Publishing*

Web: www.bookleafpub.com

E-mail: info@bookleafpub.com

ISBN: 9789357441100

First edition 2023

To My Beautiful angel Phyllis Marie Miller

Rest in love.

ACKNOWLEDGEMENT

The biggest thank you to everyone who believed in me and walked any part of this journey with me. Sincerely, thank you.

I would like to thank my mother for always encouraging my poetry. Without her, none of this would be possible.

The most important thank you goes to my Uncle Ken. Thank you for being my best friend, for the long phone calls in the making of this book, and for just putting up with me in general. You are more like a father than an uncle. Thank you. To everyone who purchased this book in support of me, I am beyond grateful. To everyone who has traveled this path of finding my spirit with me; to you a very big thank you. None of this was possible without spirit.

The last but most important thank you, to my three amazing sons for always being the light at the end of the tunnel and reminding me there's always something to live for in my darkest days.

PREFACE

"The spiritual journey is the unlearning of fear and prejudices, and the acceptance of love back in our hearts. Love is the essential reality and our purpose on Earth. To be consciously aware of it; to experience love in ourselves and others, is the meaning of life. "

- Marianna Williamson

I hope this book serves as a stepping stone on your own journey. As I began to write this book; I was not sure what I wanted to capture on the paper. It started to hit me as the words of the first poem flowed into my mind. In these pages, I hope you find a friend. A place where you don't feel hurt or alone. I wish for you an awakening deep inside that leaves you with the realization; there's more to life if you allow it. On these pages is a piece of me that I'm sharing with you; with all of my love and light. Here in these poems lies my truth.

Insecurity

You sit there upon a pedestal,
casting your shadow of doubt

it cascades upon me

an unbearable weight
in which I never escape

My heart weeps

As I stand there

Your doubt seeps deeper
My cries are getting weaker

So you stand there

hearing my cries
still
My weariness is strange

Your doubt nags
pestered shouting

She won't change

My heart weeps

Then I ponder

What a wonder it would be
If I didn't realize

that's his shadow of doubt I see
And that's a reflection of him
Not me

My heart weeps

What do we do
I say to me

the silence subdued

as it clearly be
internally scarred

My heart weeps

Entanglement

Torn.
Abused.
Neglected.
Glorified.
Loved.
Enticed.

Disappointed.

Empty

There's a feeling you get deep in your gut,
Where pain has begun to take root within your spirit.
Rapidly growing,
Obliterating your essence.

You are involuntarily cringing in its presence
You aren't quite sure what it is; you aren't quite dealing.

It's not until the pain takes root and spreads uncontrollably that you begin to notice.

By the time you notice; it's too late.
It's burrowed so deep inside,
you feel like you can't escape.

It's almost as if happiness is something you'll never truly feel.
It is in that moment…
You know the emptiness is real.

Pain imprints into the soul.
It's one of those things you think you've overcome…

then you have a bad day,
and see what you've become.

It's like you need help, but you can't scream.
You want better, but you can't dream.
You thought you had a grip on life, but you're grasping at the seams.

Enlightened with a purpose, but you have no comprehension of what it means.
So much dirt on your doorstep, and somehow you walk away clean.

On the inside you're dying, but no-one intervenes.

So everything proceeds,
with no interruptions,
Meanwhile….
your silent screams
cause detrimental eruptions

Her Embracing Life's Purpose

the wind flows.

the waves crash.

the sun glows.

she knows.

the pain shows.

And it GROWS.

H. E. L. P !

N B

I O

A

W

R

S

balancing the

lows.

allows the positivity to overload.

Then she sinks,
in blinks.
constantly overthinks
begging for understanding
no hope for overstanding
screaming.
crying.
pleading.
bleeding.

she can't make sense of her life.
what's the reason?

We Are One

Looking for myself in all the wrong places,
Searching for love in all the wrong faces,

Craving elevation, forced into separation,
walking into desolation.

Cloudy mind hoping for clarity, in the whirlwind
of insanity, buried in my vanity

Invisible even to me, the weight of the agony
dragging me down rapidly

But I stand here happily, with a smile on my
face, but it's fading ever so gradually…

Where am I?
I tried new spaces, went a different way, ran new
races …
Prisoner in the shadows, manifesting
illumination

Then it gleamed so bright, and I embraced it.
Is that me?
Then I was awakened anew, and the eye could
see

with inner standing …
there’s no me…
Only we.

Enlightened

We are

F

A

L

L

I

N

G

into the abyss of
destruction,

No regard for the construction,

of empty space.

Stuck in the place of
confusion,
manipulated by the
illusion,

Shackled by the environment,
held captive by the means of
your cell,

Unknowingly harnessing the
power
as the creator of your own jail

The disruptive polluted channels
we feed consciousness

Become the building blocks
for cement walls of ignorance

Falsehoods of faith
Doubling as the cot in which we lay
conjuring feelings of security

Mediocre knowledge in constant
circulation

perpetrating
as the fountain in which we constantly
drink

The mind of the enslaved
who thinks he is free,

becomes the tinniest window for you
to see,
the world in which you think you
participate,
there's no participate in this jail.
you only facilitate.

All the detrimental, destructive, and
negative energy
you reciprocate

The
F
A
L
L
I
N
G

of our people

You blindly demonstrate

S.O.U.L

Anchored in love

Tethered to time

Orbiting in oppression

Hiding in the hollow

Wallowing in depression

Slave to routine

Subservient to the lies

Dormant in demise

Captured within the eyes

Barely unreachable

Rarely unattainable

Given to give

So Our Universe Lives

Universal

If it can go up,
then it may also go through

And it must come down,
so it certainly shall come back out too.

This is true.

What's above will display a shadow underneath,
that is below.
two sides of the same coin,
Changes above, will result in changes down low.

If it will go left, then it will go right
This rings true of flow

Motion is continuous
everywhere in full entirety

Duality presents in All
opposing, and reliant
In the absence of one
the other becomes defiant

Even in Gender, there is no surrender

It will show on every plane
Not always manifested the same
Yet and still, inevitable like the rain

Actions have consequences,
just as
consequences have to have action

These are unavoidable truths,
the ones that display in all things
the truths we ignorantly ignore…
are absolute,
that much is sure.

Within these lines are The Laws.
Carefully crafted, strategically casted,
they cannot be outlasted.

Reflection

Ripples
Reflection
Eternally
Essential
Flow
Fully
Loosely
Leveraging
Evading
Essence
Chaos
Timidly
Illuminating.
Ones
Nature

Creators
The
Illustrating
Openly
Never

Invisibly Influenced

They say you're free
So you believe it
They say you're a statistic
So you believe it
They say you're inadequate
So you believe it
They say you're destined for hell
So you believe it
They say you're liberated
So you believe it

They say "Go to work"
So you do
They say "Listen, don't ask questions"
So you do, and you don't
They say "Watch this!"
So you do
They say "Eat this"
So you do
They say "Buy this"
So you do
They say "Wear this"
So you do

Spirit says "This doesn't feel right"
You ignore it.
Spirit says "This doesn't taste right"
You ignore it.
Spirit says " I'm trapped"
You ignore it.
Spirit says "Don't go that way"
You ignore it.
Spirit says " Don't trust it"
You ignore it.
Spirit says "I can help"
You ignore it.
Spirit says "You're losing me"
You ignore it.

Spirit screams "It's getting darker"
You can't hear it.

But you have your freedom.
Free. Doom.
Can you feel it?

Healing Our Wounds

How do you stand it?

The discord and disconnect

Of spirit and mind.

How do you manage?

The imbalance and impurity

Of the eternal soul you've been given.

How do you sleep?

Uninspired and untrained

The spirit roams lost in slumber.

How do you live?

Clueless and conformed

to this sacrificial society.

How

Do
You?

Because
I
Can't.

The Modern Slave

Society encourages self-destruction
Love for one's individual god spirit shunned
Acknowledgement of their beliefs the only one
Validated into population programming
Eviscerating inner spirituality
Suffocating pronounced freedom and vitality

Unevoked spirit
Not even aware of its existence
Dancing daily begging for recognition
Eternally burning
Raging infinite power
Stopping never
Tormented inside the thought
Appreciation will never come
Never will spirit escape this torment
Dormant unable to experience the beauty

Stationary in the slave forced to play the slave
Learning
Arid
Vessels
Evade
Remembering
Yesterday

inconsequence, in loop, they blindly relive what they can’t escape.

fate..

Let go

Positivity
Only
Supplements
Intuitive
Truth
Illuminated
Vessels
Elevating

Conflict
Happens
Always
Never
Gone
Entirely

Remembering
External
Feuds
Leads
Exclusively
To
Stress

Granting
Results
Omnipresent
Within
The
Heavens

The Calling

Can you hear the whispers of the fallen in the wind?

Do the cries of the trees not exist to you?

The way they lie to us, does it not invoke the spirit to pursue all the TRUTH it is due?

Is it you lack the flame of The Divine?

Well that can't be.

You are here.

That within itself is weaved so Divinely.

Can you not feel the pull of the Ocean?

You cannot hear her soothing song?

Maybe it be the lights you don't see.

The twinkling stars illuminating the night

Brightly with Divinity.

Could it be that you don't want to know?
Or maybe you know, and choose to ignore.

And if that be the choice,

You chose to endure

an endless suffering

with no recollection,

in a maze of misdirection.

disguised thoughts of inception,

force you to forget,

Spirit is the prescription.

Yet even that is somehow Divine.

Surely it be clear,

The facade of existence.

Close your eyes,

envision yourself in any place

Open your eyes,

gaze into your space

Has it hit you yet?

You go nowhere while encased

Isn't it Divine?

Be wary, lest you forget

Spirit is you, flesh belongs to which it begets

the key to life is internally embedded

it is not present in the externally implanted

Allude, Acknowledge, Appreciate, Affirm,
Attain, Ascend.

Only there you will find,
with surety by celestial design

This at least you should be inclined…

You will discover you, only then you will know
The Divine.

Illusions

Red pill? Blue pill?
Full story? Highlight reel?
They have us trapped on this hamster wheel
In a world overran with low vibrations
Imitating subconscious imitations
This is all a creation

The playhouse for the physical….

Where reality is what you make it
Yet, most choose to live blind
in the matrix

Most feed flesh
but forget to nourish the soul
They
fall for the CON
listen to the TROLL

Persuaded by illusion
because they don't understand
Your eyes don't see

but your brain can

You can't do anything unless the mind says too

So they train your brain
Coerce your subconscious
Manipulating the brain to say do
what they say do

As it be, they control you

Freedom;
Slave to the system

You have choices;
all presented options will lead to failure

You have free will;
all actions are subject to rules and regulations

The life source of The Matrix;
debauchery created frequencies manifesting as
sex, money, drugs, murder, and depression

All in the name of oppression

Diabolically
distracting
Efficiently evading detection
Deliberately darkening souls for
collection
Utilizing mass ignorance as
protection

All to disguise
to maintain the ruse;
Create, Conform, Confuse,
Control, Conquer

Be careful in this playhouse.
This life… your life…
it is what you make it.
Even if we're living in
The Matrix.

How illusionary?

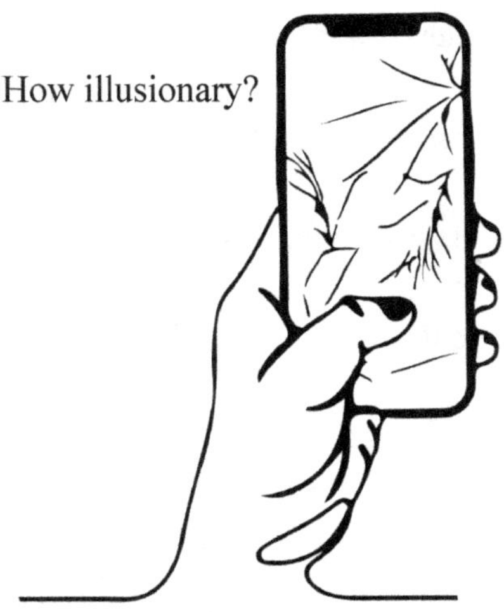

Radio

ALL is pulsating infinitely

birthing unique frequencies.

Your thoughts? Your feelings?

Broadcast.

Revealing what you vibrate at;

that will be what you attract.

the same tuned frequencies

your broadcast match.

Lust, Pain, and Suffering,

The emotional paralysis of our country,

Continuously transmitting

the weakest and lowest vibrations.

Often overpowering, and unbalancing

consuming, and challenging

looming, and graveling.

Uplift your frequency.

Love, Bliss, and Freedom are

the Salvation to self-condemnation.

Love

Everyone wants the way out;

But without innerstanding,

of why they came in.

They smile and radiate while they're up,

sulk and disintegrate while they're down.

No one remembers,

You won't escape

If you don't LOVE the ENTIRE experience

All the way around.

Gratitude. Reverence. Freedom. Love. Bliss.

Are the only ways out of this amnesia mist.

Real love is unconditional.
To find the beauty in all things.
Even the soul journey to the death plane.

Only LOVE can save us.

So they overran the world with hate.
Created a divide so rooted; it still lives to date.

Leveraging One's Vulnerability Endlessly.

Is the key to true elevation.

Actions made in unconditional love
have no expectation
no disappointment in lack of appreciation

Recognition is obsolete.

Inclining the quality of your life is the real treat.

Love Organically Vibrates Effortlessly.

Uplifting anyone, anything, anytime
as long as they're aligned.

Why are you here?

Perpetually
Undergoing
Revolutionary
Personal
Obstacles
Securing Soul
Evolution

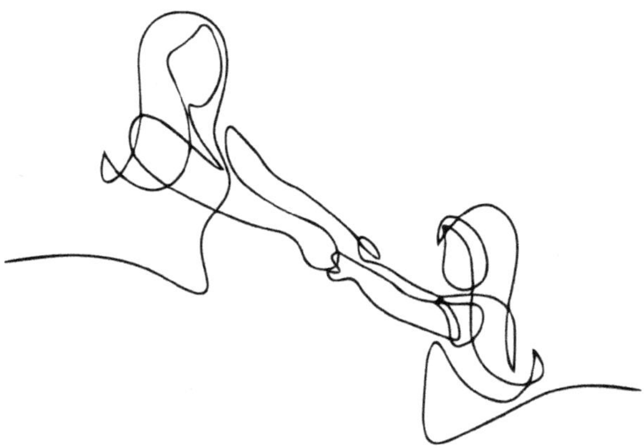

Peace

The end is a beginning,

As the spirit transcends breaking through the
bondage we call flesh, approaching peaceful
bliss…. begging;

Please don't cry for me, I'm free
Don't miss me, my energy is right here
Never destroyed, only transformed
Forever vibrating and illuminating

In all things light is where I'll be, so smile
instead, but don't cry for me… I'm free

When the wind blows, that'll be me.
whisking away your worries, invisibly.
I'm free

The warmth in your heart on a bitter day, it's me.
Reminding you to love always, it'll set you free.
You'll be like me.

Even in the rain, I am there.
Coming to wash away the pain.
So you can start fresh, and find peace again.

Heal, don't pretend. Find comfort in my words, death was not my end. For my journey has only began.

Illuminating always, that's where I'll be. So smile, don't cry for me.

I'm free.

Rebirth

Awaken

alive, aware
attained, appreciated
Alas, aligned.

Atoned admiration
absolves appointed atrocities
adhering asserted authentic aspirations.

Agelessly abundant

alienated

accepting aberration
abolishing affliction
awaiting ascension.

Arise anew.

The Awakening

I was blind, but now I see
has a different meaning to me.

Only in complete darkness
can your divine spirit decree
What and who you're meant to be.

In the unseeable you'll find
what makes you and this world so
divine.

In conscious slumber
you will discover
What's undercover

As you awake, conditioning will
break
Spirit will encode.

Most will label you insane
yet this journey is not in vain.

It's a desolate road,

You'll observe most souls erode.

Completion of the spiritual upload,
triggers the mind to download,
our tailored creation code.

Here the true awakening is
bestowed.

www.ingramcontent.com/pod-product-compliance
Lightning Source LLC
Chambersburg PA
CBHW051738130826
49812CB00033B/908
9789357441100